Selling on E

The Beginner's Guide: How to Sell on Ebay

By Brian Patrick

You May Also Want To Explore Brian Patrick's Best Selling Amazon Guide:

Selling On Amazon: How You Can Make A Full-Time Income Selling on Amazon

Table of Contents

Introduction   4

Getting Started on eBay   5
Becoming a Registered User   5
Signing Up For PayPal   6
Finding Your Way Around   6
Understanding the Auction Page   7
Placing a Bid   8
My eBay   10

Get Started Selling   13
What Do You Need In Order to Sell?   13
What Will You Sell?   13
Sourcing Inventory   15
Understanding eBay Fees   16
eBay Stores   18
Before You List   18

The Selling Form   19
The Short Selling Form   19
Categories   20
Using The Title Effectively   20
Item Specifics   22
Bring Your Item to Life With Pictures   22
Writing a Description   25
Format and Duration   28
Selling Multiples   31
What's It Worth?   32
Payment Methods   32

Shipping Details ... 33
Return Policies ... 38
Adding Extras ... 39
Submitting the Listing ... 39

Managing the Auction ... 40
Revising Your Listing ... 40
Answering Questions ... 41
Canceling Bids or Ending Your Auction Early ... 42
Relist Your Item ... 43
Auction Software ... 43

Closing the Deal ... 45
Receiving Payment ... 45
Shipping ... 46
Troubleshooting ... 47
Taxes ... 48
Safety and Security ... 50
Feedback ... 51
Conclusion ... 51

Introduction

Welcome to the exciting world of eBay! Selling on eBay can be both fun and profitable. eBay can be a great way to pare down your collection, clean out your closet, or sell items from your existing business. Many eBay sellers generate a regular income of tens of thousands of dollars per month. Building a business of this size takes time and experience, but if that is your goal, it's certainly possible to achieve.

Whether you've never visited eBay before, or already have some experience under your belt, the tips included in this guide will help you become a more effective eBay user. This book is designed to further your knowledge, give you confidence, and guide you step-by-step through the process of buying and selling.

In this book, you will begin by building a solid foundation – registering for eBay, and learning how to browse and search through the millions of listings available on the site. Even if you never plan to make a purchase here, as a seller it's important to put yourself in your buyer's shoes when posting an item for sale. Then, we'll give you tips and strategies for how to sell on eBay effectively, leaving you well prepared to become a successful seller.

Getting Started on eBay

eBay has more than 100 million active users – and more than 112 million items up for sale every day. That makes it the world's largest online marketplace! The first step to joining this active community is by registering as an eBay user.

Becoming a Registered User

You don't have to be a registered eBay user to browse the listings, but you do have to register before bidding, buying, or selling. Many of the features on the site are only available to users who are signed in to their eBay accounts. If you've never been to eBay before, this should be your first step. Registering is fast, easy, and free! Visit the Registration Page to get started. Ebay will ask for your name and address. You'll also be asked to choose a User ID and password.

During the registration process, eBay will ask you if you want to create a seller's account at that time. You can come back to this later, if you wish, but you'll need to complete it before listing your first item. As with the regular eBay registration, opening a seller's account is free. To register for a seller's account, complete the sections requesting your credit or debit card and checking account information. You'll then be asked to select which method you prefer for paying eBay for fees you incur during the selling process. We'll discuss these fees in more detail later. Choose whichever method is more convenient for you.

Signing Up For PayPal

Once you have an eBay account, you'll also want to sign up for PayPal. PayPal is the payment service used to buy and sell on eBay. As a buyer, this service enables you to pay for your purchases without revealing personal information such as your bank account number or credit card number to the seller. As a seller, PayPal allows you to accept credit card payments quickly and easily for all of the items you sell on eBay.

Registering on PayPal takes just a few moments. The site will ask for your contact information. You'll also need to link your PayPal account to your bank account, debit card, or credit card -- known as "funding sources." This is where the money will come from when you pay for an eBay purchase.

Finding Your Way Around

Take some time to get acquainted with eBay's categories, especially if this is your first time using the site. There are more than 20,000 categories of goods on eBay. Categories are like departments in a store, making it easy for browsers to shop.

Begin on eBay's homepage (www.ebay.com). You'll see a number of different categories displayed on the left side of the page. Clicking on one of them will take you to the homepage of that category, with subcategories displayed on the left side of the page. Explore some of the categories that interest you. You'll find that they are very specific – there are separate categories for everything from Transformers action figures to women's shoes to pocket watches. Once you've selected a category, you will be taken to a page with all of the active listings in this subcategory. Among the listings, you'll notice some with fixed prices, and others that are auctions.

Not only can you browse the many subcategories, but you can also conduct a keyword search. A bar at the top of most eBay pages gives you an opportunity to enter search terms. From the search results page, you can narrow your search by price, condition, buying format, and lots of other preferences listed on the left side of the page to find exactly what you're looking for.

As you explore the eBay site, you might also want to familiarize yourself with the site map (http://pages.ebay.com/sitemap.html), which contains direct links to many of the pages you'll be visiting as you become an active eBay user.

Understanding the Auction Page

Clicking on the title of any listing found in your search results will take you to a page of additional information about the item. This includes up to 12 photos, as well as the description provided by the seller. This is also where you'll find information about shipping costs, as well as the reputation of the seller.

When you purchase an item from a department store, you probably don't read every detail on the package. Buying on eBay requires you to do your homework. The sellers listing items here may not be professional advertisers. It is your responsibility to read the item description thoroughly before you bid. The seller's responsibility is to describe the item as best as he or she can, but not all descriptions are equal – and some are inadequate. It is important to ask questions if you don't understand the description or if there is missing information.

If you see a current listing that you're interested in watching until the end, click the "Watch This Item" link, near the top of the listing page. It will then be found in the Watching section of your My eBay page, which saves you from having to search for the item again.

Placing a Bid

Even if you plan to just sell on eBay, it is wise to buy a couple of small items to experience a complete transaction. It is also a good idea to start building your reputation by getting some positive feedback next to your user ID. When you find an item you want to bid on, read all the details and compare completed auctions to see what others like it sold for. Then you must decide how much the item is worth to you.

At the top of the auction page, you'll see a box where you can enter your maximum bid. Once you click 'place bid' a screen will pop up for you to confirm your bid. If there is a Buy It Now choice for this listing, that will be indicated near the top of the page. You can choose to click Buy It Now (and pay the seller's stated price) instead of bidding on an auction-format listing.

If you place a bid and are immediately outbid, you may wonder how it happened so quickly. There may be another person bidding against you at the same exact time. It is more likely, however, that eBay made a proxy bid for the current high bidder. The high bidder placed a maximum bid that was greater than yours, so the current bid was automatically increased. Proxy bidding can be difficult for new eBayers to understand, since live auctions don't work the same way.

As a bidder, you decide the maximum you're willing to pay, and then you type this amount. eBay then confidentially bids up to your maximum amount, but only as much of your maximum bid as is necessary to maintain your position as the high bidder. That way, you don't have to keep an eye on your auction as it unfolds.

eBay reminds all bidders that their bid is a binding contract. If you decide you don't want the item after you've placed a bid, you are still obligated to purchase it. Bids may only be retracted in a few special circumstances — and buyer's remorse isn't one of them.

My eBay

My eBay is your place to see everything you're doing on eBay. Like the dashboard of your car, it displays everything relevant to your activities in one place. If you've been an eBay member and haven't taken advantage of this section, you'll wonder how you lived without it. There, you can track your buying and selling activities, send and receive messages with other eBay members, and update your account information.

Many eBay members go straight to My eBay after signing in. This page is accessible only by you, with your User ID and password. It is an invaluable organizational tool and timesaver. There's a link to My eBay at the top of every page on the site.

There are four tabs at the top of your My eBay page. Choose the

Activity tab to see items you're bidding on and items you have listed for sale. Are you wondering whether you've received payment for an item you sold, or whether you were outbid on an auction? You'll find that information here.

In the *Sold* section of the *Activity* tab, you'll see everything you need to complete your transaction with your buyer. You can send an invoice, send a reminder note, see if they paid you, purchase postage, and leave feedback. As an eBay seller, you'll find yourself returning to this page over and over.

If you've received a message from eBay or other eBay members, you'll get a copy at the email address linked to your eBay account. A copy will also show up in the *Messages* tab of My eBay. This is similar to your email inbox.

To see or change your account information, click the *Account* tab. This is where you can change the email address associated with your account or pay your eBay fees.

Finally, the *Applications* tab hosts a number of optional, third-party applications designed to help you with your selling activities. These apps are designed to help sellers improve their efficiency and increase their profits. Subscribing to some of these apps is free, while others are paid services.

Get Started Selling

Though the selling process is more involved than buying, it's not necessarily more difficult. Actually, selling has never been easier. No need to get a business license, or rent a storefront or even a booth at your local swap meet. The seller's fees are a lot cheaper than your local newspaper ad, and eBay provides all the tools you need to advertise and list your items, post your photos, and troubleshoot any problems that may arise.

Being a seller on eBay takes many forms. You may sell one item, an ongoing stream of various items, or the same items continuously – perhaps the same items sold by your brick-and-mortar storefront, for example. You can work at your own pace, take vacations when you want, and sell on your time.

What Do You Need In Order to Sell?

Selling on eBay requires very little in the way of investment. Before you begin selling here, you'll want to invest in a good digital camera – the one on your cell phone might not cut it. You'll also need a digital scale to calculate shipping weights. We'll discuss this in more detail in the photography and shipping sections below.

What Will You Sell?

Of course, there's one other thing you need in order to sell on eBay

– inventory. Fortunately, eBay is a one-stop shopping mecca where almost anything can be bought and sold. New and used, the selection here ranges from rare antiques to kids' clothing to vacation homes. There are few limits to what you can sell on eBay. Always remember the old adage that your trash is someone else's treasure.

Do you have collectibles you want to sell but don't know where or how to sell them? Is your garage too full to park your car, cluttered with good stuff you know others could use? Are you tired of giving away your quality items for almost nothing at garage sales? Did you just inherit Grandma's attic, and now you don't know what to do with all the wonderful old treasures? Do you have a business that you'd like to expand by appealing to a larger market? You are in the right place. The reason for selling on eBay is different for everyone, but we are sure that you can relate to at least one of the above reasons.

If you're new to selling on eBay, it's best to start with things you already have around your home. That way, it won't cost you anything initially to sell on eBay. Minimal investment means minimal risk. Starting small is also a good way to build up your feedback rating – which makes you appear more trustworthy to potential bidders. Many new sellers do jump in by posting dozens of listings all at once, but it's usually better to start slowly and build up your business over time.

There are very few things that can't be sold on eBay. If you're wondering about whether the items you wish to sell are allowed, check the prohibited items policy, here: http://pages.ebay.com/help/policies/items-ov.html. If you inadvertently list something that is prohibited, your listing will likely be canceled.

Sourcing Inventory

As your business grows, you may be wondering where to find inventory. If you've already sold everything that you weren't using around your home, then you're going to need to find a new supply of goods to keep your eBay business alive. There are a number of strategies used by eBay sellers. Here are just a few ideas to get you started:

1. Thrift stores
2. Garage sales
3. Estate sales
4. Discount and outlet stores
5. Government surplus
6. Local auctions
7. Clearance racks at high-end department stores

8. Wholesale lots being sold on eBay
9. Sell the same items on eBay that you sell through your retail storefront.
10. Dropshipping. A dropshipping arrangement involves an agreement to sell items that are fulfilled by another company (the dropshipper) in exchange for a portion of the proceeds.
11. Trading assistant – sell for friends or family for a percentage of the sale price.

Many eBay sellers find it best to "sell what they know." If you're already a collector or hobbyist in a particular area, consider selling those types of items on eBay. For example, there are sellers who focus on nothing but Barbie dolls, or fishing lures, or designer handbags. By selling something you already know about, you'll have the best opportunities to find good deals and describe items accurately.

No matter where you find your treasures, make it a point to always check your item carefully for any rips, tears, chips, nicks, or other flaws. Broken zippers or a chip on the rim of a vase will quickly eat into your profits.

Understanding eBay Fees

Now that you've begun to browse eBay, you may be wondering whether there are fees to use the site. As a buyer, there are no fees to use eBay. The only fees charged by eBay are the responsibility of the seller. Sellers on eBay enjoy low overhead when compared with running a retail store, but there are still a few costs involved. Here are the standard selling fees:

http://pages.ebay.com/help/sell/fees.html

These fees are billed once per month. You can pay the bill with a credit card or through PayPal.

The basic fees for selling on eBay include an *insertion fee* and a *final value fee* (or FVF).

The *insertion fee* varies based on whether the listing is an auction or a fixed price. Sellers receive free insertion fees for their first 50 auction-style listings per month. After this number, the insertion fee ranges from 10 cents to $2, depending on the price and category of the listing.

The *final value fee* is a percentage of the total amount of the sale (including the item itself and shipping charges). It ranges from 7% to 13% depending on the category where the item was listed, as well as the sale amount.

There are additional fees for optional upgrades available during the listing process. For example, if you want to make your title stand out, or you want your auction to run for an extra-long 10 days, there are small charges for these upgrades.

You'll also want to take into account *PayPal fees*, as the vast majority of eBay transactions are paid through PayPal. In most cases, this fee is 30 cents plus 2.9% of the total amount of the sale.

eBay Stores

Are you planning to run a part-time or full-time business on eBay? Will most of your listings be fixed price, rather than auction format? If so, an eBay Store may be right for you. Ebay stores have an additional monthly fee, but lower per-item insertion fees, which makes this an economical option for those listing dozens or even hundreds of items a month. There are several subscription levels, ranging from $15.95 to $299 per month.

Before You List

Before you list your item, make sure you'll be able to present it in its best light. Wash glassware, and make sure fabric items are wrinkle-free. If it has a cord, coil it and secure it with a twist tie or wire. If the item has several parts, make sure you've gathered all of them.

The Selling Form

To post an item on eBay, start by clicking the "Sell" link found in the upper right corner of most eBay pages. You will be prompted to sign in to your eBay account, if you're not already signed in. If you haven't already signed up for a seller's account, you'll need to do so now.

Now, you're in the selling form. This page is where you'll fill in all the details about the item you're selling. Here, we'll go through the steps one at a time. You can practice filling in this form as many times as you'd like. You can even save it for another time if you're not ready to finish it now. Before posting your listing, you'll be able to preview it and see exactly what it will look like on eBay, and you'll always have a chance to revise before submitting your listing. eBay wants your item to look good and sell just as much as you do.

The Short Selling Form

There are two different selling forms you can use to list an item on eBay. The form with more choices (or the *long form)* provides all of the available options; most experienced sellers use this one. There is also a shorter, basic form that provides fewer options. It's good for beginning eBay sellers, but doesn't provide as much opportunity for customizing your listing. The form available to smartphone users via eBay Mobile is very similar to this form.

We don't recommend either of these methods (the short form or mobile form) for listing on eBay. Though the long form can take some time to get used to, making your listings truly your own is one way to increase your sales. Even with the long form, it's easy to fill in the information and submit a listing. You can change back and forth between the short form and the long form at any point in the listing process, using a link found in the upper right corner of the selling form.

Categories

Now, get started by selecting a category in which to list your item. If you're not sure where to list your item, do a search on eBay for items similar to yours, and note the categories in which they were listed. You can also enter keywords to have eBay select categories that may be appropriate, or browse the list of categories to find one that is a good fit for your item.

You also have the chance to choose a second category. If the item fits in more than one category and you believe the extra exposure will help you sell it, then it may be worth it to double your listing fees to list in two categories. However, in most cases it's not worth the extra fee.

Using The Title Effectively

Begin by writing the title of your ad. The first thing people see when you list your item is your title. Think of it as a great newspaper headline. You have 80 characters; use them wisely. You will have a better chance of attracting buyers if you include pertinent information in your ad title.

The goal here is to use all of the words that buyers might use when searching for your item. This includes the brand, the type of item, the model name or number, and the year it was made. Be sure to include more than one keyword if you think people may search for the item in different ways. For example, if you're listing a tie, include both necktie and tie.

Include condition, if the item is new or mint, but don't write used. Remember that the ad title is your way of getting potential bidders to click on your listing, so it should make your item look as attractive as possible.

Avoid using words like "RARE" or "LOOK" or extra punctuation such as dollar signs, as this takes up space without adding anything of value to the listing. Double-check your spelling – if the name is not spelled correctly, no one will find your listing using the keyword search.

Item Specifics

The next step is filling in the item specifics. This information is dependent on the category in which your item is listed. For example, in clothing you'll be asked questions about brand, size, and material. In electronics, you'll be asked questions about whether or not the item is in working condition. Item Specifics are important because they help buyers narrow down a search.

Bring Your Item to Life With Pictures

The next step is adding photos to your listing. On eBay, a picture is truly worth a thousand words. You don't need to be a great photographer to take pictures for your eBay auctions. If you are selling on eBay, all you need is a camera that can take a decent picture. You don't need a fancy, professional-quality camera. Nearly any digital camera currently on the market will work for eBay sales purposes. On the other hand, if your only digital camera is on your cell phone, you'll probably want to invest in an actual camera.

On eBay, all listings are required to have at least one photo, though you're given room for as many as 12. No matter how good your description is, a picture reinforces your presentation, and a good photo answers many questions. All 12 images are free, so use as many as possible, giving buyers every possible view of your item. A general rule of thumb is to take your photos like there's no description, and write your description like there are no photos.

A picture communicates several things to a potential buyer:

Your item really exists!

The size, proportion, color, and dimension of your item.

The close-up details of your item.

Any imperfections in your item, not always easy to describe.

Stock Images?

Many eBay sellers do use stock photos as the sole images of their items. However, eBay buyers prefer to see the actual item being sold. Otherwise, it's difficult to judge the condition of the actual item being sold. It's best to take your own photos of the items you're selling.

Here are a few tips for taking top-quality eBay photos:
- Clarity is crucial. There's nothing worse than a blurry, out-of-focus picture. If you're not too steady with your hands, consider using a tripod.
- Lighting is also critical. If you're taking photos at night, use plenty of lamps to illuminate your item.
- Forget fancy backgrounds. Move your item to a blank wall, hang it on a door, or lay it on a plain-colored towel or

blanket. You want your buyers to be able to see your picture clearly and not wonder what all the stuff in the background is.

- Multiple images. Make sure that your photographs show the item from as many angles as possible, as well as closeups of any important parts, such as a crucial detail or a damaged area.
- Capture details. If you take the picture too close, the flash might wash out or overexpose the object and make details impossible to see. Take two or three shots at different distances, and choose the best one. Many cameras also have a macro setting—it usually appears as a flower or tulip on the dial. Use this setting if you want to photograph small text, a small item, or a small detail of a larger item.
- Size matters. If you have an item that is very small or very large, take a picture of something next to it that everyone recognizes. For example, a penny, a soda can, or a 12" ruler can be used for size comparisons.

Adding a photo of your item is easy, whether it's still on the memory card in your camera or is in a folder on your computer. Either way, you'll click the Browse button in the photo section of the listing form. From there, choose the location of your photo. Make sure that they're cropped to remove anything distracting from the background. Rotate the images, if needed. Once you've selected the images, you can use eBay's tools to edit the photos, if needed. When you're ready, click Upload. This will ensure that your photos can be seen by anyone viewing your ad.

Writing a Description

Now, you'll have a chance to provide a written description. If the description is well written, it will contain all of the information potential bidders need to make their decisions. Many sellers also use this opportunity to include their sales policies, though much of that is covered elsewhere on the selling form.

There are four basic steps to writing a good ad. First, make some notes about the make, model, color, size, fabric, dimensions, and condition (good and bad) so that you don't forget to include the size of your quilt or what year your book was printed.

Second, if you know any history of your item or you'd like to explain why you're selling it, tell your buyers. Many people like the personal touch. Third, weave the facts and the historical and personal data together in an interesting way. Fourth, check your spelling and punctuation. Make sure that your ad says what you want it to say and that it looks great!

You have unlimited space to describe your item in the description box. The more information you include in your description, the fewer questions you'll have to answer by email during the auction. However, ads that run on and on lose a potential buyer and take a lot of time to write. Again, use the newspaper format. Include all the important information in the first paragraph. If you want to further elaborate, let your buyers decide if they want to read on. Many sellers use a bullet or list format which is easy to read and very effective.

To accentuate the positive, give the potential buyers reasons to buy your item. Reveal any flaws or wear that may affect the quality or beauty or your item. If you don't disclose the negative aspects of your item, the nondisclosure can come back to bite you. You may be forced to deal with a return, or have to deal with negative feedback.

Encourage lookers or bidders to check out your other auctions or your store. While you're at it, tell your potential buyers about your terrific feedback, or write about yourself or your interests in your About Me page. eBay does forbid you to mention your Web site in your auction listings, although you may put a link to your Web site on your About Me page.

You'll see as many styles of descriptions as there are sellers. Some use very fancy titles in boxes, different colors and fonts, and include more information than most are willing to read. Some will include only basic information and use simple formatting. The most effective ads anticipate the buyers' questions and include at least one clear picture. Anything more than that is up to the seller's interest in creating a unique ad. When browsing eBay, take note of what attracts you because that may be how you want to stylize your ads.

Formatting Your Listings

Have you seen fancy listings on eBay, with borders and a rainbow of text? You don't have to be a computer whiz to make your listings stand out. Ebay gives you these tools right from the listing form. You can enhance your listing by using the tools that you see at the top of the description box to change the font size, color, and other attributes. You've probably seen them in Microsoft Word or other word-processing programs that you have on your computer.

It doesn't take much to make your ad stand out by changing the text size, color, and style. Start the description with a title in a larger font size and a different color, repeating the listing title. For the body of your ad, you'll probably want to change your font size to 2 (10 pt) or 3 (12 pt). Make sure your font and color are easy to read.

A word of caution: Keep your listings professional. Avoid using text-speak and mixing too many colors or fonts, which can make the text difficult to read.

All of these formatting options are also available via HTML coding. The HTML tab is useful if you know how to format using this language. The standard way of changing your text that eBay provides is so easy, don't worry about HTML unless you already know it.

Format and Duration

For each item you sell on eBay, you must make some decisions on how to price it. Auctions aren't the only way to do business on eBay. On eBay, you have two main pricing strategies (also known as listing formats) available to you: auction format, and fixed price. Pricing will vary with your items – though you may decide that you favor one strategy over another, one size doesn't fit all.

The first is an *auction* format. You'll select a starting bid (which can be any amount, from a single penny on up). Bidding will progress over a set period – 1, 3, 5, 7, or 10 days. There is an additional 10-cent charge for sellers to list a 10-day auction. The most common time span for an auction listing is seven days, but there are reasons why you might choose to list an item for a longer or shorter period of time.

If you list your item very close to a holiday and the buyer might need it in a hurry, choose one, three, or five days. This will limit your exposure, but your ad will be closer to the top of the search results page sooner. If your item is hot and you have several of them and want to turn them over quickly, choose one, three, or five days to increase the number of sales. If you have a pricey item that would only appeal to a select group of people, then consider listing it for 10 days for maximum exposure.

At the end of the auction, the high bidder will purchase the item. You are obligated to sell for the winning bid, even if it's less than you'd hoped to receive for the item. The only exception to this is if you list your item as an auction-style listing with a *reserve*. A *reserve price* is an amount that bidding must reach in order for you to sell the item. For example, if your reserve is $78 and the bidding only reaches $55, you're off the hook. You'll have the option to add one during the listing process. However, a word of caution: many bidders pass over items listed with a reserve, because they don't like the idea of bidding against an unknown price. Adding a reserve price does come with an added fee, in order to encourage sellers to use it sparingly. So don't use a reserve if your ultimate selling price won't cover the cost. In other words, save your reserve pricing for higher cost items. If you're thinking about adding a reserve, it's usually best to just enter that amount as the starting bid.

Many eBay sellers start their auctions at $1. Starting low can be a good strategy because bidders tend to get involved in the item pretty quickly. Now, hopefully, the bidding won't stop at $1 and you'll have lots of people bidding the item up to its value or beyond. However, this is a risky strategy, especially if you are a new seller without a lot of experience. It's often a better idea to start the item at the lowest price you'd be willing to accept for it. That way, even if you only receive one bid, you'll be happy with the sale price.

The second type of eBay listing is a *fixed price* format, also known as a Buy It Now listing. These run for 3, 5, 7, 10, or 30 days. You can also post a fixed-price "Good Till Cancelled" listing, which means it automatically renews every 30 days until the item sells. These listings operate more like a retail store, in that the seller sets the price. You can choose to add the *Best Offer* feature to these listings. That means that the item will be available at a fixed price, or potential buyers can submit an offer for you to review. You're not obligated to accept their offer; you can accept, reject, or send a counteroffer.

There are pros and cons to each listing format. Auction format is generally best for items that you believe will generate a lot of interest, such as rare collectibles. Meanwhile, fixed price listings tend to work best for commodities and situations where there may be dozens of similar items posted on eBay at a given time. In addition, if your profit margin is low, listing with a fixed price can protect you from having to sell for lower than your cost, which is a possibility with auction format listings.

Another convenience eBay offers (but charges for) is the option to list your item at another time. If you're up late at night and finish your listing, you may want to schedule your listing to begin the next day, when more people will be up to see it.

Selling Multiples

Do you have more than one identical item? Duplicates can be sold on eBay in several ways:
- A fixed-price listing with a quantity of more than 1. This enables your buyers to buy one, or more than one, of the items at a time. The listing is active until the time has run out or all of the items have sold, whichever comes first.
- Auctions and a Second Chance Offer. Once you've sold the first item via an auction listing, you can offer the duplicate item to the second bidder, for the same price. Sometimes,

however, they've moved on or lost interest, in which case you'll need to click the Relist button in order to sell the second item.

What's It Worth?

What is your item worth? Sometimes pricing takes time and research. As a seller, you don't want to set your price too low and lose out on profit. Yet you don't want to price your item so high that it doesn't get any attention or bids.

Using Completed Listings

Though you may know how much you paid for it, this may be pretty far off what it's worth to an eBay buyer. You can use eBay's Completed Listings search (which looks at the past 90 days of eBay sales) for an idea of what the item is worth. From the search results page, select the *Completed Listings* option from the left side of the page. This search shows you listings that have ended within the past 3 months. It gives you a good idea of what you can expect to sell your item for. Savvy eBay sellers always use this tool when deciding how to price their items.

Payment Methods

On eBay, PayPal is by far the most common payment method. In the payment section, enter the email address you used to set up your PayPal account. This isn't necessarily the same email address linked to your eBay account. You can also choose to accept other electronic payment methods, such as Skrill, ProPay, or credit cards through a merchant account you already have.

eBay does have restrictions on the payment methods sellers are allowed to accept. Although money orders and personal checks were once commonly used to pay for eBay purchases, eBay's current policy is that sellers are not allowed to ask buyers to send money orders or checks for purchases except in a few select categories, such as Business and Industrial.

Shipping Details

The next step in the listing process is entering the shipping details. Before you sell an item, you must have a shipping plan. Many new sellers find this to be the most challenging part of listing their item on eBay. How could you possibly know what the item costs to ship if you haven't taken it to the Post Office?

Most people have had limited experience shipping items from their homes. Where to get shipping supplies, how to weigh and pack the item so that it arrives safely, what to charge and which service to use can be daunting when you think about selling on eBay. There are many choices to make.

In order to calculate shipping costs, you'll need to know both the weight and dimensions of the package. Heavier packages may be weighed on your bathroom scale, but lighter packages will need a different approach. If you have an accurate food scale, you can use that for lightweight packages. Some post offices have a scale in their outer lobby for your use, though this is time-consuming. When you feel you can't operate without a scale any longer, purchase a digital scale. It's an investment you'll have to make sooner or later. You'll find a digital shipping scale to be invaluable when calculating the weight of your item.

Which kind of digital scale will work best depends on what you plan to sell. Some sellers find that one with a 5 pound weight limit is adequate, while others opt for a 30-pound or even 75-pound scale.

Always weigh the item in its box and packing materials so you'll know how to calculate shipping.

Shipping Materials
Save all the bubble wrap, packing paper, and Styrofoam that comes to your house and recycle it in your packages. It's free and environmentally friendly. Ask friends, family, or co-workers to save packing materials and you may never have to purchase anything. If

you do need more, make sure you check out supplies on eBay—they're usually more reasonably priced than in stores. If you buy at the post office or a shipping store, you will likely pay top dollar, but sometimes if you're pressed for time, it is worth the few extra dollars.

Shipping Methods

If you have a small item that weighs less than a pound, USPS First Class is often the best option. It is relatively inexpensive and relatively fast. Larger items are most often sent via USPS Priority Mail. If you plan to use Priority Mail from the post office, the U.S. Postal Service will deliver boxes of several sizes right to your door.

If you have an item that is relatively heavy for its size, and it fits into a Priority Mail Flat Rate box, you'll often save money by using one of these. They are special boxes with a set postage price based on the box you're using, not its weight or destination. Although they aren't very large, if you are shipping something small and heavy, you'll save money with the flat rate shipping.

If you are shipping CDs or books, you can use the Media Mail rate. It is much cheaper, but you need to know the service is very slow. It can take up to six weeks for your item to reach the buyer. However, it's often quite a bit cheaper than comparable shipping methods, especially if you're sending a whole set of books.

All of these services are offered by the US Postal Service. Your other two options are FedEx and UPS. These services tend to be quite a bit more expensive when shipping small, lightweight items (particularly those that qualify for USPS First Class). If the items you're selling are larger, UPS or FedEx may be an affordable option. Also, many sellers find that it's better to use UPS when shipping a fragile item. In case of breakage, they handle claims quickly and efficiently, unlike USPS that has much paperwork and is slow to refund insurance money.

Flat Rate Shipping

Flat Rate (or Fixed Price) shipping is great for items that can be sent USPS First Class (which means they weigh less than 13 ounces). If you use the fixed shipping cost option, estimate the maximum shipping cost by using the ZIP code of the farthest-away place you'll ship your item to, such as a state on the other side of the country.

Calculated Shipping

The *Calculated Shipping* option is a good idea for items that are particularly large or heavy. Shipping charges for these items will vary greatly based on the distance they are traveling. By using eBay's shipping calculator, you can display rates to the buyer's zip code. Potential buyers can see your shipping rates even before they bid.

To use calculated shipping, enter the weight and dimensions of the box, and select the shipping service(s) you wish to use. If you wish to charge your buyer more than the actual shipping cost, you can add a dollar amount into the 'handling fee' box. The buyer will not see this extra handling charge; they will only see a total amount for shipping & handling.

Free Shipping

It is becoming increasingly common for sellers to offer 'free shipping.' It's not really free, of course – it's just added into the price for which you've listed the item. This is best for small, lightweight items – the type you could use Fixed Price shipping for. Calculate the cost to ship the item to the furthest shipping destination, and add this to the price you'd like to charge for the item itself, to calculate the total amount you should ask for the item.

Shipping Internationally

Your next choice is to decide whether to sell only in your country, to sell selectively to certain other countries, or to sell worldwide. Should you ship internationally? Many sellers do, while others don't. If you're new to the idea of regularly shipping packages across the country, shipping internationally can be a bit intimidating. New eBay sellers may be better off restricting their sales to U.S. audiences until they are more comfortable with the idea of shipping internationally. Selling worldwide isn't difficult, but it requires more time and attention to details.

If you do choose to send your items abroad, the process is much the same as sending items within the U.S. During the listing phase, you'll use the same weight and box dimensions you used for domestic shipping. You'll then select the international destinations you're willing to ship to, and the shipping service(s) you wish to use. The most commonly used are USPS Priority International and USPS First Class International, which is offered for weights up to 4 pounds.

Return Policies

Finally, it's time to set up your return policy. eBay has made it easy to specify your return policy with just a few checkmarks, such as the length of time the buyer needs to make their decision after receiving the item, and whether you or the buyer will pay return shipping. Take a few minutes to decide your return policy details so there's no guessing or assuming on your buyer's part.

Adding Extras

The next section is the promotional section, where eBay tries to convince you that the more features you have, the better your item will sell. You can pay extra to use a subtitle, make your title stand out with bold text, or add a background or border to your listing. Look the options over and decide if any meet your needs for this listing. The prices are upfront to let you know what the cost will be. In our experience, these costs are only worth it if your item is particularly valuable.

Submitting the Listing

Now, you're done with the listing process. Click Preview, and you'll be able to see what the listing will look like. You'll also see your listing fee, including any of the special features you selected. At each section, you can click Edit to change anything in that section. If everything looks the way you want it, click List at the bottom of the page, and your listing will be posted on eBay.

Managing the Auction

Now that your auction is live, it's time to sit back and watch the bids come in. Don't forget to check back in regularly. You may receive questions from potential bidders while your listing is live. These messages are forwarded to your email address, and also found in the My Messages section of My eBay. Always respond to these questions promptly; if you wait too long, you could miss out on a sale.

Revising Your Listing

Have you suddenly realized that you forgot to include dimensions, or wish you'd taken another close-up photo of your item? Even when you double-check your seller's form, you might forget to enter some important information, or you might make a mistake. Though there are a few limitations, it's simple to revise or add to your auction.

Before the bidding begins, and within twelve hours of the auction's end, you may do the following:

- Modify your item title or description.
- Change your minimum bid price.
- Change your item's category.
- Add, modify, or remove a reserve price.
- Add or modify the Buy It Now price.

- Change shipping terms.
- Update payment methods.
- Add or change your images.

If your item has already received a bid, or is close to the end, your options are more limited. At this point, you may only add to your description, add item specifics or upgrade to more selling features.

To revise your listing, open the item via your My eBay Selling page. At the top of the auction page, click the Revise link. You'll be taken to the selling form. Some of the sections will be grayed out; this means you can no longer edit them.

Answering Questions

If you omit information about size, weight, dimensions, or other pertinent information about your item, interested bidders will email you. When there is a question, you will receive a message from the potential bidder through eBay. You have the option of answering them privately or having eBay post your answer on your listing page, eliminating the need to answer the same question repeatedly. It is quicker than revising your auction, and you'll notice that many sellers do this. However, some readers may not find your update, so many sellers also add this information to the description of their item.

When you respond to your potential buyers, answer their messages quickly so that they have ample time to bid. Be specific and polite, and indicate your willingness to provide any extra information.

Canceling Bids or Ending Your Auction Early

You probably will never cancel any bids, because as a seller you want your item to receive as many bids as possible. If you find it necessary to cancel bids on your auction, eBay insists that you provide good reason to do so because they allow cancellations only in specific instances.

For example, if you are concerned that your bidders are not serious about buying your item, contact them via an eBay message to verify their intentions. If, after several attempts, you do not hear back from them, you may cancel their bid without their consent.

You also have the option to end your auction early, though eBay discourages this. Remember that many bidders wait until the last hours to bid. However, in certain instances – such as if the item has been lost or broken since you posted the listing – you can cancel your auction.

If you need to cancel a bid, click the Site Map tab at the bottom of any page. Under Sell, click Cancel Bids or End Your Listing. Provide a reason for canceling bids or ending an auction early.

Relist Your Item

In the event you don't sell your item the first time it is listed, you can relist it without doing all the work over again. Click *Relist*, located on your auction page or in your My eBay 'Unsold Items' section. Frequently, the item will sell the second time around. Remember that every day there is a new audience on eBay.

Auction Software

If you find that you are selling more and more items on eBay, it may be time for some extra help. Many sellers who have made eBay their full-time job have help from software designed to ease their workload. Don't sign up for these programs just yet. Many eBay sellers find that once they're comfortable selling items through eBay itself, they don't see a need for such programs, since My eBay provides many tools for managing your sales.

Ebay's own services, including Turbolister and Seller's Assistant, are here to help. So, too, are many third-party programs designed to help eBay sellers, such as Auctiva. Some are more user-friendly than others. The costs vary, too. Some of the services available through such programs include:

1. Bulk uploading – Write as many of your ads as you want at one time, then send them to eBay at the same time.
2. Manage shipping labels and invoices
3. Automate your communications with buyers
4. Track inventory

Closing the Deal

Congratulations! Your item has sold! What now?

At the end of an auction, the buyer will receive an email directing them to pay for their purchase. As long as you've filled out all of the shipping information when posting the listing, this is a streamlined process. In most cases, buyers are able to complete the transaction through PayPal without any need to contact the seller directly. In fact, many bidders pay immediately – especially on Fixed Price listings.

When your items sells, you can utilize your My eBay to complete the transaction. In the Sold section of the Selling page, you'll see everything you need to begin your communication to your buyer. You'll see at a glance if your buyer has paid by PayPal. If you haven't received payment yet, send the buyer an invoice. This is done directly from My eBay, too.

Receiving Payment

When the buyer pays, you'll receive an email from PayPal, and the item will be marked as Paid in My eBay. The payment will be in your PayPal account. If you haven't received payment a day or two after the end of the auction, send a second copy of the invoice to the buyer. This serves as a payment reminder. You could also send the buyer a friendly message – via eBay Messages – to remind them to pay.

If you have not received payment within 4 days of the sale, you should file an Unpaid Item claim. Most buyers will pay at this time, but if you still haven't received payment in 4 additional days, close the claim. You'll receive your eBay fees back, and will be free to relist the item. This step also notifies eBay that the buyer has not paid; if the buyer has a pattern of nonpayment, eBay can suspend their account, making eBay a better place for everyone.

Shipping

Now that the item has been paid for, it's time to ship it to the buyer. When packaging your item, remember to include a copy of the invoice in the package and pack it securely so it will survive its trip.

Many new eBay sellers make the mistake of standing in line at the post office, waiting to mail their items. This is time consuming, and it's also more expensive than buying postage online. As long as you have an accurate scale (or only use USPS Priority Flat Rate boxes, whose postage doesn't vary by weight), you can buy postage online, and drop the packages off at the post office without waiting in line. You can even schedule a free pickup, so you won't even have to leave the house to ship the items. By buying postage through eBay and PayPal, you receive Commercial Base rates, which are about 10% lower than the rates you'd get at the post office.

Buying postage online is easy. Once the item has been paid for, visit My eBay. A selling reminder near the top of the page will tell you how many items you have to ship. Simply follow the prompts to enter the weight and dimensions of the package, and choose a shipping service. Your buyer's shipping information is automatically entered. Once you pay for the postage via PayPal, you can print out a label to tape to the box.

A tracking number will be automatically uploaded to eBay, letting the buyer know when to expect their package. This tracking number is an important component to shipping the item. If the buyer claims they never received the package, this tracking number is used to determine whether the buyer is due a refund.

Troubleshooting

It is eBay's philosophy that people are basically good. The majority of eBay transactions are pleasant and rewarding for both the buyer and the seller. In any transaction, however, there is a small chance that either party will end up unhappy. eBay has many safeguards to ensure your transactions go smoothly, and many ways to resolve problems if they arise.

Good communication is one key to a successful transaction. Courteous, direct messages ensure that buyers and sellers receive positive feedback after the transaction is complete. If your buyer is having an issue, you may receive a message from them. In some cases, buyers go straight to the Resolution Center and file a claim. There are 2 main types of claims you'll be concerned about as a seller: Item Not Received (INR) and Significantly Not as Described (SNAD).

Item Not Received
If your buyer says that the item they ordered has not arrived, the first step should be checking the tracking number. Does the tracking number say the item has been delivered? If not, does it appear to be on its way? Often, letting the buyer know when to expect their item to arrive is enough to quell their fears. You are responsible for making sure the item reaches your buyer, or refunding their money.

Item Not As Described
No matter how carefully you look over an item before listing it, it's always possible that you overlooked something. The item may also have been damaged while in transit. In either case, it is best to have the buyer ship the item back to you, and refund their money. Note

that on eBay, sellers are responsible for ensuring the item reaches their buyer safely. Regardless of whether you purchased shipping insurance, you'll need to refund the buyer's money if it arrives broken.

Returns

Many sellers accept returns for any reason. Others stipulate that returns are only accepted if the description was wrong. If a buyer wishes to return an item, it's often in your best interest to let them – otherwise, you may end up with negative feedback if they aren't happy with the item, even if it wasn't your fault.

Taxes

The fun part about selling on eBay is making money! The money you make from your eBay sales, unfortunately, is taxable income. It is taxed just like any other income earned. Neither eBay nor PayPal is in the business of reporting your income. Therefore, they do not submit any forms to the IRS. If you're concerned about figuring out potential tax liabilities for your eBay sales, the best thing to do is to speak to your tax advisor about all of your income and expenses when you make money on eBay.

Some eBay sellers are also responsible for paying sales tax. Within the listing form, there is the option to charge sales tax to your buyers. Do not charge sales tax unless you are responsible for paying sales taxes to your state. Again, speak to your tax advisor if you have any questions about income or sales taxes when selling on eBay.

Safety and Security

Many people who are new to the idea of selling online are concerned about their security. With so many stories in the news about identity theft, it's easy to become overwhelmed at the thought of putting your personal data online. Here are a few things to keep in mind when buying and selling on eBay:

PayPal Protects Your Banking Information
One of the most valuable aspects of sending or receiving PayPal payments is that the site prevents your personal information from being seen by your trading partner. When you sell on eBay, your buyer won't see your credit card or bank account information – only your email address. The same is true when you're buying on eBay.

eBay's Buyer and Seller Protection Policies Work For You
Before you begin selling on eBay, be sure to read these policies thoroughly. They are here to protect you.

All Messages From eBay Appear In 'My Messages'

Have you received an email purportedly from 'eBay,' and you're not sure if it's legit? Check My Messages. If it appears there, it's legit. If not, forward the email to spoof@eBay.com. They can tell you whether the message is truly from eBay, but chances are, if it's not in My Messages it's spam.

Feedback

Feedback is what gives buyers and sellers their reputation in the eBay community. The final step in the transaction is leaving feedback for your buyer. Ebay only allows sellers to leave positive feedback. As long as the transaction went smoothly, you should leave a positive feedback for the buyer. Often, this prompts the buyer to leave one for you, building up your rating. Leave feedback within 90 days of the sale date.

Conclusion

You're on the road to becoming a good eBay seller! We want your sales to be successful. As you continue on your journey as an eBay member, we wish you the best of success. We hope we ignited a new eBay flame by giving you the tools to become a savvy eBay seller. By now, you have a good idea of items you could sell on eBay, and how to sell them effectively. We want you to continue to find interesting items to sell, and wish you smooth transactions with your buyers.

GrassRootBooks.com Publishing

GrassRootBooks.com is a boutique publishing firm that specializes in publishing fiction and non-fiction books. We have a number of high-quality works currently available on the Amazon Kindle Store.

Check out our site and join our newsletter for updates on our latest books, free book promotions, and upcoming releases.

www.grassrootbooks.com/newsletter

At GrassRoot Books, we work with both accomplished and up and coming authors, partnering with talent and producing high quality works. Check out our homepage at www.grassrootbooks.com

Copyright Note:

This book is for personal use only. No section of this book may be copied, reproduced or republished in any form without the written consent of the publisher.

Printed in Great Britain
by Amazon